Spiritual Happiness in the Midst of Adversity

Spiritual Happiness in the Midst of Adversity

Cindy Isler

Spiritual Happiness in the Midst of Adversity

Chosen Destiny Books

Copyright © 2021 Cindy Isler

All rights reserved. No part of this book may be used or reproduced by any means, graphic, electronic, or mechanical, including photocopying, recording, taping or by any information storage retrieval system without the written permission of the publisher except in the case of brief quotations embodied in critical articles and reviews.

Unless otherwise noted, Scripture are taken from THE HOLY BIBLE, ENGLISH STANDARD VERSION (ESV): Scriptures taken from THE HOLY BIBLE, ENGLISH STANDARD VERSION ® Copyright© 2001 by Crossway, a publishing ministry of Good News Publishers. Used by permission.

Scriptures marked NIV are taken from the NEW INTERNATIONAL VERSION (NIV): Scripture taken from THE HOLY BIBLE, NEW INTERNATIONAL VERSION ®. Copyright© 1973, 1978, 1984, 2011 by Biblica, Inc.TM. Used by permission of Zondervan

Scriptures marked NKJV are taken from the NEW KING JAMES VERSION (NKJV): Scripture taken from the NEW KING JAMES VERSION®. Copyright© 1982 by Thomas Nelson, Inc. Used by permission. All rights reserved.

Scriptures marked NLT are taken from the HOLY BIBLE, NEW LIVING TRANSLATION (NLT): Scriptures taken from the HOLY BIBLE, NEW LIVING TRANSLATION, Copyright© 1996, 2004, 2007 by Tyndale House Foundation. Used by permission of Tyndale House Publishers, Inc., Carol Stream, Illinois 60188. All rights reserved. Used by permission.

Scriptures marked AMPC are taken from the AMPLIFIED BIBLE Classic Edition (AMPC): Scripture taken from the AMPLIFIED® BIBLE, Copyright © 1954, 1958, 1962, 1964, 1965, 1987 by the Lockman Foundation Used by Permission. (www.Lockman.org)

Scripture quotations marked TPT are from The Passion Translation®. Copyright © 2017, 2018 by Passion & Fire Ministries, Inc. Used by permission. All rights reserved. ThePassionTranslation.com.

Dedication

This book is dedicated to 3 beautiful women in my life. My aunt Esther, my best friend since fifth grade, Minister Sonya Lewis, and my girl Theresa Gill Jones. These amazing women have been with me on my journey through every trial, disappointment, loss, win, high and low. They loved me when I didn't love myself. They have prayed with me and prayed for me. They kept me encouraged when I could not encourage myself. From my heart, to each of you beautiful ladies, I will always love you and appreciate you.

Philippians 1:6 Be confident of this, that he who began a good work in you will carry it on to completion until the day of Jesus Christ. (NIV)

Definitions

Adversity – difficulties, misfortune, mishap, calamity or distress.

Happiness – a state of well-being and contentment.

Growth – the act of process or a manner of growing, development, gradual increase.

Peace – freedom of the mind from annoyance, distraction, anxiety, an obsession, etc. Tranquility, serenity.

Spiritual – relating to people's thoughts and beliefs, rather than to their bodies and physical surroundings.

Happiness – good fortune, pleasure, contentment and joy.

Cindy Isler

When Life Takes Over

We all go through things in life. Some things are expected, and some unexpected. There are some people that cannot handle when life comes in and takes over. They can't handle being blind-sided and caught off guard. But unfortunately, that is a part of life, and life will throw you some curveballs.

The question is, will you catch those curveballs or do you let them knock you down? Do you allow life to consume you and send you in a downward spiral, or do you go toe to toe with it. Do you command that mountain to move or do you stay in that state of depression and anxiety.

What do you do when life takes over? Here are some scriptures to meditate on while going through all that life throws your way.

Jeremiah 29:11 "For I know the plans I have for you," declares the Lord, "plans to prosper you and not to harm you, plans to give you hope and a future." (NIV)

Jeremiah 31:3-4 The Lord appeared to us in the past saying: "I have loved you with an everlasting love; I have drawn you with unfailing kindness. I will build you up again, and O Virgin Israel, will be rebuilt. Again you will take up your tambourines and go out to dance with the joyful." (NIV)

Psalm 18:16-19 He reached down from on high and took hold of me; he drew me out of deep waters. He rescued me from my powerful enemy, from my foes, who were too strong for me. They confronted me in the day of my disaster, but the Lord was my support. He brought me out into a spacious place; he rescued me because he delighted in me. (NIV)

Psalm 32:8 "I will instruct you and teach you in the way you should go; I will counsel you with my loving eye on you." (NIV)

Psalm 46:10 "Be still and know that I am God." (NIV)

Cindy Isler

Below, take a moment and think about a time when life happened and took over. Below, write down a few and how you handled it.

_____
_____
_____
_____
_____
_____
_____
_____
_____
_____
_____
_____
_____
_____
_____
_____
_____
_____
_____
_____
_____
_____
_____
_____
_____

Spiritual Happiness in the Midst of Adversity

Cindy Isler

Adversity

Adversities are inevitable! There are many types of adversities that we may encounter in life. We may encounter financial adversity, social adversity, health adversity, death of a loved one, a breakup, job loss, etc. Yes, events happen all the time that are beyond our control.

Adversity is not intended to come and take us out. It is very important how adversity is handled when it shows its unwelcoming face. It is not the end of the world when challenges come.

This is why it is important to have a close relationship with God. His words tell us that He will never leave us nor forsake us. You are not exempt from the promise that was made to all of God's children. Sometimes you may hear people say *look on the bright side of things*, but in the midst of adversity, I am sure the bright side is not what you see. Stop focusing on the problem and just see yourself through the situation.

Proverbs 24:10 If you faint in the day of adversity, your strength is small. (NKJV)

Philippians 4:12-13 I know how to be brought low, and I know how to abound. In any and every circumstance, I have learned the secret of facing plenty and hunger, abundance and need. I can do all things through Him who strengthens me. ESV

Spiritual Happiness in the Midst of Adversity

2 Corinthians 12:9 But He said to me, "My grace is sufficient for you, for My power is made perfect in weakness." Therefore I will boast all the more gladly of My weaknesses, so that the power of Christ may rest upon Me. (NIV)

Romans 8:28 And we know that for those who love God all things work together for good, for those who are called according to His purpose. (ESV)

James 1:12 Blessed is the man who remains steadfast under trial, for when he has stood the test he will receive the crown of life, which God has promised to those who love Him. (ESV)

Isaiah 45:7 I form light and create darkness; I make well-being and create calamity; I am the Lord, Who does all these things. (ESV)

Cindy Isler

Out of My Control

I know by now you are probably thinking, *this woman really doesn't know what she is talking about,* but you are wrong. I have experienced many unavoidable adversities that were out of my control.

Just to share a little bit about me, when I was 20 years old, my mom and aunt were killed while on vacation in Virginia Beach. The last words that my mom spoke to me before leaving for her trip were, *are you still coming.* I was planning to drive down later to spend time with the two of them. She told me that she loved me and that she would see me when I arrived.

Well, that never happened. They had already been killed before I arrived. I had no clue how drastically my life was about to change. I didn't know what I was walking into. I would never see my mommy and Aunt with life in them ever again.

When I arrived at Virginia Beach, I did not know where my family was so I went to see Kevin, who was a family friend. I left his home and went back to the condominium where they were staying and still, there was no mommy or auntie to be found.

I fell asleep in the car waiting for them to come back. As I waited, a gentleman woke me up because I was blocking a trash can. I explained to the man I was looking for my mom and I couldn't find her. It just so happened that he stayed across the hall from my family and was able to let me into their condominium.

I went inside and looked around to make sure everything was ok. I laid down and went to sleep. Shortly after, the gentleman comes back and knocks on the door asking me when was the last time that I had spoken to my mom. I went over to his condo and called my dad and asked him if he had talked to mommy. He responded saying no, asking me what was wrong. I replied and told him I couldn't find her.

The gentleman had a private conversation with my dad while I sat in his living room talking to his daughter. I waited patiently but eventually I asked if my mom had been killed. He never mentioned that there was an accident and that two women had been killed. He called the police and they came to talk to me.

My mom and aunt did not have identification on them but my mom did have keys. The police were going to the parking lots trying to see if the keys would allow them entry into any of the cars. The officer said to me, *I am sorry but your mom has passed.* He asked if I wanted to see pictures but I told him to wait until my family arrived.

This news was known halfway across the country before my family ever knew about it. I could have never imagined that the next time I would lay eyes on my mom and aunt they would be laying in a casket looking like angels.

I called my friend Saul who lived close and he came to sit with me while I packed up my mom and aunt's belongings. My family arrived and we all went back to Arlington, Virginia where we lived. That was the longest drive ever.

Cindy Isler

A young man who was in his early twenties hit my mom and aunt with his car and fled the scene. My mom and aunt both flew in the air and were both killed. Their bodies were so broken up that they couldn't wear regular clothes for the funeral. The young man turned himself in much later.

There were items pertaining to drugs and alcohol found in his vehicle. He was sentenced to 1 year in jail for hit and run and was found not guilty for involuntary manslaughter.

Every 20 year old need their parents and I never knew that my mom would depart her earthly life to enter her eternal life at such a young age. I know that God knows what is best for all of us. I needed my mom, but God needed her more.

My sister Dawn and I were introduced to Sunday school and singing in the choir at a very early age. My mom would normally work on Sunday's a lot, but she always made sure we were in Sunday school and that we attended church. I had a close relationship with God at an early age which helped me to deal with my loss and heaven's gain. It did not decrease the pain, but I never went in a downward spiral. That experience groomed me into the woman that I am today. The bible is a source of strength, giving people courage to face life's most difficult challenges.

Psalm 31:24 Be strong and let your heart take courage, all you who wait on the Lord. (KJV)

Psalm 138:3 On the day I called, you answered me; my strength of soul you increased. (NIV)

Matthew 11:28 Come to me, all who labor and are heavy laden, and I will give you rest. (NIV)

Spiritual Happiness in the Midst of Adversity

Psalm 119:28 My soul melts away for sorrow; strengthens me according to Your word! (NIV)

Psalm 119:50 This is my comfort in my affliction, that Your promise gives me life. (NIV)

Psalm 62:6 He only is my rock and my salvation, my fortress, I shall not be shaken. (NIV)

Isaiah 40:29 He gives strength to the weary and increases the power of the weak. (NIV)

Psalm 29:11 The Lord gives strength to His people; the Lord blesses His people with peace. (NIV)

Cindy Isler

Most of us have lost a loved one. Some may have lost a loved one tragically, or you may have been able to spend time with your loved one before they transitioned. Use this page and write down how you handled your loss. Were you angry? Did you feel like God was punishing you? Did you slip into a depression? How did you handle your loss? What could you have done differently?

_____
_____
_____
_____
_____
_____
_____
_____
_____
_____
_____
_____
_____
_____
_____
_____
_____
_____
_____
_____
_____
_____
_____
_____

Spiritual Happiness in the Midst of Adversity

Cindy Isler

Prayer

    My God, My God, You know my story and You know my pain. You knew all of the losses that I would have to endure in this life. I needed my mom, but You needed her more. You are the parent above all parents, and I thank You for being my mother and father. I thank You for every low place and every high place. I thank You for wrapping Your loving arms around me when I did not understand the why's in my life. Thank You for calling me your daughter. In Jesus name I pray. Amen

Growth in Adversity

When our mothers birthed life into us they knew we would not remain babies forever. They knew we would endure challenges in life and face adversities. They also knew that we would grow up and mature into men and women.

Well, the same goes for God. We are His children and He wants us to grow and mature into the men and women that He is calling us to be. He already knew the challenges that we would encounter, as our life story has already been written. Growth in adversity allows us the opportunity to have a closer relationship with God.

Adversity is not to punish, but sometimes it happens to get our attention. What you do in the midst of adversity is totally up to you.

Ephesians 4:15 *Instead, speaking the truth in love, we will grow to become in every respect the mature body of him who is the head, that is, Christ. (NIV)*

2 Peter 3:18 *But grow in the grace and knowledge of our Lord and Savior Jesus Christ. (NIV)*

You can either look at adversity as a setback, or you can use adversities as a lesson that helps you to grow into God's will for your life. You must learn how to grow through your pain. Adversity is for a reason and you have to try and understand God's purpose for it.

During your adversity, you are reminded of your weakness. This is because God always wants you to remember that He is the source of your strength. We often operate on our own strength, and this is when we get tired and weary.

It is not smart to go through life without asking God for guidance and direction. You can't go through life with a spirit of arrogance thinking that all of your success and accomplishments are all because you did it alone. God has a way of keeping us balanced so we can keep our eyes on Him.

God is so faithful to us. He is dependable, trustworthy and reliable. There are always lessons in the pain that you go through. Everything that you go through *is* for a reason. Although you may experience pain, and you may be misunderstood, you have to learn how to rest in God. Trust the promises that He has made to you.

Going through adversity will force you to trust God, or not trust Him. Lean and depend on Him, or run in the other direction. Your choice. But God wants us to grow and mature spiritually. You may see the adversity that is going on around you but God is dealing with us internally. One of His goals is to mature us spiritually. Below are a few scriptures for you to think about and meditate on.

Romans 5:3-5 We can rejoice, too, when we run into problems and trials, for we know that they help us to develop endurance. And endurance develops strength of, and character strengthens our confident hope of salvation. And this hope will not lead to disappointment. For we know how dearly God loves us, because he has given us the Holy Spirit to fill our hearts with his love. (NIV)

Spiritual Happiness in the Midst of Adversity

Romans 6:23 For the wages of sin is death, but the free gift of God is eternal life through Christ Jesus our Lord. (NLT)

Romans 8:28 And we know that god causes everything to work together for the good of those who love God and are called according to his purpose for them. (NLT)

2 Corinthians 1:3-7 All praises to God, the father of our Lord Jesus Christ. God is our merciful Father and the source of all comfort. He comforts us in all our troubles so that we can comfort others. When they are troubled, we will be able to give them the same comfort God has given us. For the more we suffer for Christ, the more God will shower us with his comfort through Christ. Even when we are weighed down with troubles, it is for your comfort and salvation! For when we ourselves are comforted, we will certainly comfort you. Then you can patiently endure the same things we suffer. We are confident that as you share in our sufferings, you will also share in the comfort God gives us. (NLT)

2 Corinthians 12:7-10 Even though I have received such wonderful revelations from God. So to keep me from becoming proud, I was given a thorn in my flesh, A messenger from Satan to torment me and keep me from becoming proud. Three different times I begged the Lord to take it away. Each time he said, "My grace is all you need. My power works best in weakness, so that the power of Christ can work through me. That's why I take pleasure in my weaknesses, and in the insults, hardships, persecutions, and troubles that I suffer for Christ. For when I am weak, then I am strong." (NLT)

Cindy Isler

Prayer

  Heavenly Father, I just want to thank You for loving me. I want to thank You for making me Your masterpiece. As I went through life, and its adversities, I have grown to be the child of God that You want me to be. No matter how painful it may have been, I continued to draw closer to You and depend on You. Yes, growing pains hurt at times, but I have learned to see myself through the trials and pain. I thank You for loving me and keeping Your hands on me. In Jesus name I pray. From my mouth to Your ears. Amen

Spiritual Happiness in the Midst of Adversity

Why Me

We live in a fallen world and adversities show no favoritism. God will use the most trying times in our lives to bless us. All adversities are not bad, but it is how you respond to it.

In the midst of adversities, people often ask why me. In some situations you will never know why. Sometimes your adversities are because of you. You could be at fault, it could be because of how you have treated people, or your decisions, your sins, your selfishness or your pride. Satan hates Godly people. But God loves you even though He will allow you to go through heartache, pain and difficulties.

Power is perfected in weakness, and this is something you need to remember. We tend to disobey God and when we do, we must pay the consequences. God does things in our life to protect us but it may not look or feel like it at times. God does not send adversity into our lives to hurt us but to help us.

Always remember, you are never alone in the midst of adversities. God is always there. God wants you to see the good in every adversities. He wants to change your thought process. He wants you to stay on the path He has set before you.

Jesus experienced adversity through the harassment of His enemies who wanted to destroy Him. He also experienced adversity through the agony of dying on the cross. Adversity is brought upon us not because we lack faith or because we are disobedient, but as a way to increase our faith.

The bible says that all you need is faith the size of a mustard seed. And you can barely see a mustard seed. Some people don't even have that much faith.

Hebrews 12:4-11 You have not yet resisted to the point of shedding blood in your striving against sin, and you have forgotten the exhortation which is addressed to you as sons. "My son, do not despise the chastening of the Lord, Nor be discouraged when you are rebuked by him; For whom the Lord loves he chastens, And scourges every son who he receives." If you endure chastening, God deals with you as with sons; for what son is there whom a father does not chasten? But if you are without chastening, of which all have become partakers, then you are illegitimate and not sons. Furthermore, we have had human fathers who corrected us, and we paid them respect. Shall we not much more readily be in subjection to the Father of spirits and live? For they indeed for a few days chastened us as seemed best to them, but He for our profit, that we may be partakers of His holiness. Now no chastening seems to be joyful for the present, but painful, nevertheless, afterward it yields the peaceable fruit of righteousness to those who have been trained by it. (AMP)

Spiritual Happiness in the Midst of Adversity

Can you think of times when adversity consumed you and you did not understand why? Did you ever take a look at yourself and look back at your past actions and maybe, just maybe, this is why you are going through this adversity. Take a moment to reflect on your life on the things you did not understand. What did you do? Use the space below to write your thoughts.

_____
_____
_____
_____
_____
_____
_____
_____
_____
_____
_____
_____
_____
_____
_____
_____
_____
_____
_____
_____

Cindy Isler

Prayer

Heavenly Father, I come to You just to say, thank You. I may not have understood every trial and adversity that may have come my way, but I knew that You had me covered. As I asked myself why me, in the same sentence I had to ask myself why not me. I know that You want better for me than I want for myself. As I have become closer to You, I have learned how to deal with adversity better. So, I thank You for never turning your back on me. In Jesus name I Pray. Amen!

Cindy Isler

God Needs Your Attention

When adversity comes, we are forced to face our problems. Even those that are too big for us to resolve on our own. In this way, God gets our attention and it forces us to communicate with Him more. We have to ask God for wisdom and seek His word more, and trust that He will bring us out.

Christ's invitation becomes more attractive to those who are weary in the midst of trials and tribulation.

Matthew 11:28-30 Come to Me, all you who are weary and burdened, and I will give you rest. Take My yoke upon you and learn from Me, for I am gentle and humble in heart, and you will find rest for your souls. For My yoke is easy and My burden is light. (AMP)

Yes adversity can be long and painful but when you seek the Lord in the midst of it all it will work for your good.

John 8:47 He who is of God hears the words of God; for this reason you do not hear them, because you are not of God. (NLV)

Jeremiah 23:18 But who has stood in the council of the Lord, That he should see and hear His word? Who has given heed to his word and listened? (KJV)

Jeremiah 26:3 "Perhaps they will listen and everyone will turn from his evil way, that I may repent of the calamity which I am planning to do to them because of the evil of their deeds. (NIV)

Job 36:11 If they hear and serve Him, They will end their days in prosperity and their years in pleasures. (NIV)

Cindy Isler

Prayer

God, please forgive me for not giving You my undivided attention. I know that You are a jealous God and I don't want to put anything or anyone before You. I release everything that is not of You and I commit to You everything pertaining to me. In Jesus name I pray. From my mouth to Your ears! Amen!!!!

Spiritual Happiness in the Midst of Adversity

Hear My Cry

Adversity will cause you to cry out to God. God responds to the cry of his children when they suffer.

Psalm 34:17-19 The Lord is our Strength. "When the righteous cry for help, the Lord hears and delivers them out of all their troubles. The Lord is near to the brokenhearted and saves the crushed in spirit. Many are the afflictions of the righteous, but the Lord delivers him out of them all." (ESV)

Don't ever think that God does not see your tears or hear your cry. You are His child and He knows and feels every emotion that you have. We are to cry out to God with our voice.

Psalm 3:4 I will call out to the Lord, and he answers me from his holy mountain. (NIV)

It is ok to cry out to God for mercy every day.

Psalm 86:3 Have mercy on me Lord, for I call to you all day long. (NIV)

When we cry out to God, it is important that we cry out with humility and a pure heart.

Psalm 66:18 If I had a cherished sin in my heart, the Lord would not have listened. (NIV)

Cindy Isler

Prayer

    Thank You God, for hearing my cry. Thank You for not ignoring me even in the times that I did not listen to You. You are awesome and I love You! From my mouth to Your ears. Amen

Fear the Lord

It is important to remember that God is present at all times and that we are held accountable to Him for every thought, word and action. The word of God reminds us in Proverbs 9:10 *That the fear of the Lord is the beginning of wisdom, and knowledge of the Holy one is understanding.* (KJV)

It is very important that we never forget that God exists. God often allows painful reminders that we do need Him.

Let's take a look at Judges 2:20-22 Therefore the Lord was very angry with Israel and said, "Because this nation has violated the covenant I ordained for their ancestors and has not listened to me, I will no longer drive out before them any of the nation's Joshua left when he died. I will use them to test Israel and see whether they will keep the way of the Lord and walk in it as their ancestors did." (NIV)

Proverbs 14:27 The fear of the Lord is a fountain of life, turning a person from the snares of death. (NIV)

Proverbs 22:4 Humility is the fear of the Lord; its wages are riches and honor and life. (NIV)

Cindy Isler

Adversity Exposes Pride

Pride is the source of many difficulties and this is why it is important to do a self-evaluation. Proverbs 13:10 Tell us that *where there is strife, there is pride, but wisdom is found in those who take advice.* (NIV)

Proverbs 11:2 *when pride comes, then comes disgrace, but with humility comes wisdom.* (NIV)

Proverbs 29:23 *Pride brings a person low, but the lowly in spirit gains honor.* (NIV)

God detests pride, but humility prompts the gifts of his grace.

James 4:6-7 *tells us that he gives us more grace. That is why the scripture says God opposes the proud but shows favor to the humble. Submit yourselves then to God. Resist the devil and he will flee.* (NIV)

In difficult times our pride is exposed because it shows our need for God. In the midst of adversity, I challenge you to seek to grow in humility.

Prayer

Heavenly Father, I come to You as humbly as I know how. I come to You asking for forgiveness for my lack of humility. Please forgive me for my prideful ways. God, I want to thank You for exposing the areas in my life that need work. Thank You for being so gracious. In Jesus, name I pray. Amen and Amen.

Cindy Isler

The Armor of God

    In the midst of adversity do not be overwhelmed or give in to the temptation to give up.
    Ephesians 6:10-18 *10 Finally, be strong in the Lord and in his mighty power. 11 Put on the full armor of God, so that you can take your stand against the devil's schemes. 12 For our struggle is not against flesh and blood, but against the rulers, against the authorities, against the powers of this dark world and against the spiritual forces of evil in the heavenly realms. 13 Therefore put on the full armor of God, so that when the day of evil comes, you may be able to stand your ground, and after you have done everything, to stand. 14 Stand firm then, with the belt of truth buckled around your waist, with the breastplate of righteousness in place, 15 and with your feet fitted with the readiness that comes from the gospel of peace. 16 In addition to all this, take up the shield of faith, with which you can extinguish all the flaming arrows of the evil one. 17 Take the helmet of salvation and the sword of the Spirit, which is the word of God. 18 And pray in the Spirit on all occasions with all kinds of prayers and requests. With this in mind, be alert and always keep on praying for all the Lord's people. (NIV)*

Giving Thanks in the Midst of Adversity

Some people find it difficult to give thanks in the midst of adversity. If for no other reason at all, give thanks because God loves you and is Your Father. Give thanks because He is always there with you no matter what. Give thanks because He will help you bear the pain and get through all trying times.

When things are going your way, it is easy to give thanks. But what is your response when things aren't going your way? Don't give excuses for why your ugly attitude may be the way that it is. Learn how to have an attitude of thankfulness and gratefulness regardless of the adversity that goes on in our life.

1 Thessalonians 5:16-18 *16 Rejoice always and delight in your faith; 17 be unceasing and persistent in prayer; 18 in every situation [no matter what the circumstances] be thankful and continually give thanks to God; for this is the will of God for you in Christ Jesus. (AMP)*

I understand that being persistent and unceasing in prayer may not be easy in the midst of trying times, but it is important that you give thanks just for knowing that He will help you get through these situations. You don't have to understand why these situations have taken place. It is important to give thanks for everything because of who God is to us.

Being thankful in hard times reminds you that, you are still walking with God and He is still walking with you. Giving thanks will cause you to take a closer look at why things happen. If you are thankful, it is ok to let God know that you don't understand why these adversities are happening.

God causes all things to work together for good as is stated in Romans 8:28. God is a loving God and you have to trust him no matter what you encounter in life.

God never changes and He is the same God when things are good and when things are challenging. God wants us to have total dependance on Him. He doesn't want you to be independent when it comes to Him. He is that parent that wants you to grow up, but yet, still depend on Him.

Your pain will become more bearable when you don't focus on the situation, but focus on God. Trust Jesus as your personal Savior and watch what happens. God will walk with you through every valley. He will also mend your broken heart and He will turn your situations into something profitable for you. He will make sure your anxiety turns into peace.

Below you will find scriptures that will be helpful for you.

Deuteronomy 31:6 *Be strong and courageous, do not be afraid or tremble in dread before them, for it is the Lord your God who goes with you. He will not fail you or abandon you." (NIV)*

Philippians 4:6-7 *Do not be anxious or worried about anything, but in everything (every circumstance and every situation) by prayer and petition with thanksgiving, continue to make your (specific) requests known to God. And the peace of God (that peace that reassures the heart, that peace) which transcends all understanding, (that peace which) stands guard over your heart and your minds in Christ Jesus.* (AMP)

Spiritual Happiness in the Midst of Adversity

Prayer

God, I give You thanks for all things even when I don't understand. I thank You for turning my anxiety into peace and not letting me focus on the adversity that has come into my life. I thank You for your presence within me, and surrounding me, that will renew me physically, spiritually and emotionally. In Jesus name I pray! Amen

Cindy Isler

Spiritual Happiness

What is spiritual happiness? It can mean different things to different people. When I think of spiritual happiness, I think of being spiritually strong no matter what I am going through. I think of being spiritually happy no matter what storms are brewing.

When your marriage is falling apart you are still spiritually happy. Your mind is clear and your heart isn't weighing heavy. You aren't crying because you are in the midst of adversity, but your tears are tears of joy because of who God is to you. And God is with you every step of the way.

When your children are misbehaving, being disrespectful, dropping out of school and doing drugs, you continue to be spiritually happy. You are able to release your children, placing them in God's hands, as you continue to trust in Him. Standing in the gap for them in prayer, thanking God for their turnaround so that they walk in alignment with His Word.

There are times you can't think straight, you start feeling sick in your body, you start losing your hair because of stress and so on. You can't see the light at the end of the tunnel and it seems like your prayers aren't being answered, or even heard. You may feel like you are on an island by yourself. You disconnect from people and even disconnect from God.

Spiritual Happiness in the Midst of Adversity

Well, adversity is not meant for you to disconnect or unravel at the seams. I remember having to hold it together even when my life appeared to have tsunami after tsunami rush in. I know what it feels like to be hurt, disappointed and let down. I know how it feels to lose a parent and close friends. I know how it feels to have financial difficulties. I know how stress settles even when you don't intend to stress. At one point, my blood pressure was over 200.

God is all knowing and is so ever present.

My relationship with God became stronger and I felt closer to Him because I spent more time with Him. I cried out to Him even when I didn't have words to say. I started praying differently and I started thanking God for bringing me out. I started thanking Him for calming the storms in my life and giving me extra wisdom and guidance.

It is important to know the Word of God and start applying it to your life and to your situations. Don't let life's adversities take you down, let them build you up. It is important to have a spiritual dimension and that means finding a sense of inner peace. That includes peace of mind and peace in your heart.

Your sense of spirituality is deeply personal. Here are some scriptures that can and will help you.

Psalm 37:4 *Take delight in the Lord and he will give you the desires of your heart.* (NIV)

Isaiah 12:2 *Surely God is my salvation, I will trust and not be afraid. The Lord, the Lord himself, is my strength and my defense; he has become my salvation.* (NIV)

Isaiah 12:3 *With joy you will draw water from the wells of salvation.* (NIV)

Cindy Isler

Romans 5:2 *Through who we have gained access by faith into this grace in which we now stand. And we boast in the hope of the glory of God.* (NIV)

Matthew 5:8 *Blessed are the pure in heart, for they will see God.* (NIV)

Job 5:17 *Blessed is the one whom God corrects; so do not despise the discipline of the almighty.* (NIV)

Spiritual Happiness in the Midst of Adversity

Prayer

Thank You God, for the spiritual happiness that I have had in the midst of adversity. Thank You for the strength that You have given me and the willingness to push through. I was able to see myself through every situation the closer I became to You. I thank You for the joy and peace You have blessed me with. In Jesus name I pray! Amen and Amen.

Cindy Isler

In the midst of adversity, have you been able to have spiritual happiness? Take a moment and think back on how you felt and responded to your situation. Write it down.

_____
_____
_____
_____
_____
_____
_____
_____
_____
_____
_____
_____
_____
_____
_____
_____
_____
_____
_____
_____
_____
_____
_____
_____
_____
_____
_____

Spiritual Happiness in the Midst of Adversity

Cindy Isler

What does spiritual happiness mean to you?

Spiritual Happiness in the Midst of Adversity

Cindy Isler

There is a Reason For Everything

As I have shared earlier, I have endured a lot in my 51 years of life, but it did not break me. Even when the pain is so incredible that you can't explain it, nor understand it. I have prayed and prayed, and the more I prayed, I learned how to channel my pain. I have learned that there are lessons in every struggle.

Life happens to us all, but it is intended to strengthen us, not weaken us. Think for a moment. You made it out of that situation even when you did not see a way out. You go through things in life because God knows that you can handle them. The word *FAITH* carries a lot of weight. How much faith do you have? How much weight can you carry?

Your faith can heal and deliver you. Your faith can bring you out of situations that you thought you could not get out of. You must have blind faith baby, because faith is the assurance of things hoped for, the conviction of things not seen.

Be still and know that I am God!

Life will teach you things and it is up to you to pay attention. This is not a dress rehearsal, so every day you need to try and be a better version of you. Don't just survive in this life, you have to thrive and live your life to the fullest.

You Have Work to Do

I want you to understand that, when God brings you out of situations, it is not just for you, it is for other people. God brings you out so that you can help other people who feel like they are the only ones going through the same situation that God brought you out of.

This is why it is important to respond correctly to the situations you go through. This is why you learn the lessons and pass the test. Adversity is a classroom in which we can learn more about Christ and become more like Him.

Do you realize how important it is to be like Christ? It is very important because we were made in His image. We all have made choices, and a lot of them may not have been the right choices. With that being said, there are consequences. Consequences that may cost you something in your life. What have you learned? Did you pass the test?

Cindy Isler

You Are a Winner

The enemy has no place in your life and he is rendered powerless. Batter up, it is your turn to hit the ball out of the park. The ball is thrown at you, and sometimes you see it coming, and sometimes you don't. Sometimes you hit the ball, and sometimes you don't. The ball may knock you over and cause you some pain. Do you get back up and hit it again? Or do you just lay there.

Sometimes this is how life works. But I want you to know that through adversity you are still winning. Deal with the challenges you are faced with, and position yourself in the correct stance. You were created to win and hit the ball out of the park.

God has equipped you for the battles that you come up against. Pray, focus, and swing. You got this. Losing is not an option! Home run, baby. Then onto the world series. You have to face your challenges with faith, grace and courage. Read and repeat!

Isaiah 58:11 *The Lord will guide you always; he will satisfy your needs in a sun scorched land and will strengthen your frame, you will be like a* well-watered garden, like a spring whose waters never fail. (NIV)

Spiritual Happiness in the Midst of Adversity

Prayer

Thank You God, that I am a winner. No matter what comes my way or how hard it hits me I continue to brush it off and tell myself that I am winning. Thank You God, for courage and faith to overcome what comes my way. In Jesus name I pray. Amen & Amen.

Cindy Isler

Think about a time when you were the batter up, and the ball hit you and knocked you down. How did it feel? Did you know you were knocked down? If you did, how long did you lay there? Get up baby, and brush it off because it is time for another win. Write about your experience and how you got up and brushed yourself off and kept going.

Spiritual Happiness in the Midst of Adversity

Cindy Isler

It is Birthing Time

No one wants to be faced with adversity, but as I said earlier, it is inevitable in life. I learned to look adversity in the face and smile. I have learned to deal with adversity by accepting the challenge. I love a good challenge because I refuse to lose.

Adversity makes me use my time wisely instead of focusing on the negativity around me. Adversity has bred a lot of creativity in me as I pushed through. My pain has birthed books, nonprofit organizations, foundations, and business ventures. I have learned to use the adversities in my life as weights that have made me stronger.

I have turned my pain into purpose. We don't want to hear anything about the process because we want everything to be fast and done quickly, but the process comes before God's promise.

God has deposited greatness in each of us, and what you do with *it* is totally on you. All of us have something to offer and it is important that we are obedient and birth what God has put inside of us. We go from conception to birth in three trimesters. When a woman is pregnant with a child her body must stretch to accommodate the developing fetus. Now, because we are talking about birthing a vision, this goes for the men too.

Spiritual Happiness in the Midst of Adversity

You must stretch to be in alignment with the spirit of God. It is very important that you protect the vision (your baby) that you are carrying. You have to be careful when it comes to the midwives that you have surrounding you.

Psalm 140:4 *Keep me safe Lord, from the hands of the wicked; protect me from the violent, who devise ways to trip my feet. (NIV)*

That includes your friends, family and people that you meet. In this process God will begin to stretch you and prepare you for dilation so you can get ready for labor.

Proverbs 24:10 *if you falter in a time of trouble how small is your strength!* (NIV)

Stretching is never comfortable and not an easy task. Often, the pain and tightness of the stretching will make you feel like you can't go on. But God is with you through the entire process.

Isaiah 40:29-31 *He gives strength to the weary and increases the power of the weak. Even youths grow tired and weary, and young men stumble and fall; but those who hope in the Lord will renew their strength. They will soar on wings like eagles; they will run and not grow weary, they will walk and not be faint.* (NIV)

No matter how tough it gets DON'T abort the vision because your due date is approaching. It is important to stay on God's time-table.

Ecclesiastes 3:11 *He has made everything beautiful in its time. He has also set eternity in the human heart. Yet no one can fathom what God has done from beginning to end.* (NIV)

You must have patience to endure under pressure and waiting patiently for God's appointed time.

Hebrew 6:12 *We do not want you to become lazy, but to imitate those who through faith and patience inherit what has been promised.* (NIV)

Follow God's assignment and allow him to prepare you for labor. I know you may be scared and anxious, but just relax, God is in total control. Make sure you are spending more time with God and reading His Word.

Habakkuk 2:3 *For the visions is yet for the appointed time; It hastens toward the goal and it will not fail. Though it tarries, wait for it; For it will certainly come, it will not delay. (AMP)*

God knows that you are tired, just hold on. It is important that you have a full term delivery.

1 Peter 5:10 *But the God of all Grace, who hath called us unto his eternal glory by Christ Jesus, after that ye have suffered a while, make you perfect, stablish, strengthen, settle you. (NIV)*

John 16:21 *A woman when she is in labor, has sorrow because her hour has come; but as soon as she has given birth to the child, she no longer remembers the anguish, for joy that a human has been born unto the world.* (MEV)

Congratulations, you have gone from conception to parenthood!

Spiritual Happiness in the Midst of Adversity

Did you allow adversity to breed creativity while in the midst of your challenges? What visions or dreams did you birth? Were your labor pains painful? Who were your midwives surrounding you during the process? Did you write any books? Did you start a business? Did you start a nonprofit? Did you start a foundation? Answer the above questions below.

_____
_____
_____
_____
_____
_____
_____
_____
_____
_____
_____
_____
_____
_____
_____
_____
_____
_____
_____
_____
_____
_____
_____

Cindy Isler

Spiritual Happiness in the Midst of Adversity

Prayer

Heavenly Father, I want to thank You for the greatness that You deposited in me. I want to thank You for trusting me with the vision that You impregnated me with. Thank You for surrounding me with the right midwives. Thank You for helping me breath and push when I felt like giving up. Thank You for all of the labor pains and stretch marks to remind me of the process. In Jesus, name I pray. From my mouth to your ear. Amen and Amen.

Cindy Isler

Walking in True Purpose

Life can be so fleeting! The word fleeting is an adjective that describes something that happens really fast, or something that doesn't last as long as you would like. Driving in a car on the highway, you see a bear in the woods, but you only get a fleeting glimpse of it because you are driving fast.

A person who walks in their true purpose walks with intention, mindfulness, and they are selfless. People and opportunities chase you down. But if you are not careful, opportunities can pass fleetingly by. A lot of people have no idea what their true purpose may be. I remember asking God many times what was it that I was supposed to be doing in life? What was my purpose so that I can walk in it.

All I knew was that I wanted God to get all the glory in all that I did. God gives us different tasks in life, and we may not even understand why, but they line up with our purpose.

Exodus 9:16 *But I have raised you up for this very purpose that I might show you my power and that my name might be proclaimed in all the earth.* (NIV)

We are all different, and we all have different gifts and abilities. As we walk in our purpose our walk will look different. God has a complete blueprint for each of us and His plan and purpose for us is far beyond our comprehension.

Spiritual Happiness in the Midst of Adversity

Sometimes we have to let certain things in our lives go so that we can walk in our true purpose. Whether it is a job, a relationship or friends. And I am speaking from experience. Don't miss what your true purpose is because of the clutter in your life. If you do, it will cause you to miss what God is trying to tell you.

Sometimes it is in your waiting stage that God gives you your next steps. True purpose has been embedded in us by God.

Ephesians 2:10 *For we are God's handiwork, created in Christ Jesus to do good works, which God prepared in advance for us to do.* (NIV)

Our purpose is greater than ourselves and we must make sacrifices. No matter what mistakes you have made in the past don't allow your past to override God's promises for you.

Cindy Isler

Are you still looking for your true purpose? Are you waiting patiently, or are you rushing the process? Are you holding on to things, or people that you need to let go of? Are you willing to make sacrifices? Answer the above questions below.

_____
_____
_____
_____
_____
_____
_____
_____
_____
_____
_____
_____
_____
_____
_____
_____
_____
_____
_____
_____
_____
_____
_____
_____
_____

Spiritual Happiness in the Midst of Adversity

Cindy Isler

Prayer

Thank You God, for trusting me with my purpose. I didn't know what You had in store for me, but once I let some things go in my life, doors started opening and I began to see things a lot clearer. Thank You, for Your patience with me. In Jesus, name I pray. Amen and Amen.

Spiritual Happiness in the Midst of Adversity

Love Letter to Jesus

  I am so thankful to have You in my life. You love me despite my flaws. You have always listened to me when no one else would. You have never broken a promise to me, even when I didn't deserve for You to keep it. You understood every emotion and every tear that I have felt and cried. You have been a mother to me when my mother was killed, and You have been a dad to me when my father passed.

  Even when I turned my back on You, You never rejected me when I returned. I am glad that You never treated me the way that I have treated You. You have given extra wisdom when I asked. You have forgiven me for all of my sins, even when I couldn't forgive myself. And You threw them in the sea of forgetfulness. You paid a price for me that no one else would ever do. You sacrificed Your life for me, and I just want to say thank You.

  I want You to know that there is no other love like Yours. Even when I looked in all the wrong places it led me right back to You. I just want You to know that there is no other man before You. You are my number one man now and forever more.

Your daughter,

Cindy

Cindy Isler

Now it is your turn to write a love letter to Jesus. Pour your heart out to Him and express your feelings.

Spiritual Happiness in the Midst of Adversity

Cindy Isler

Nuggets to Fuel You

Approach adversity with determination and motivation.

Hard times presents you with the chance to change course, reinvent yourself or find an undiscovered bridge that will get you over the hurdle.

A healthy dose of optimism goes a long way when adversity occurs.

You have to approach Christ with a surrendered will, a determination to follow Christ and a firm faith in His word.

Your first response to adversity should be to open scriptures and see what God has to say to us.

God's word gives us encouragement, direction and comfort.

Adversity causes us to examine our lives.

As we turn to the Lord in our pain and difficulties, He reveals sin and wrong thinking so that we can repent, be cleansed and live a holy life.

God gives us patience to wait for His perfect timing.

Spiritual Happiness in the Midst of Adversity

God will never prolong our suffering beyond what is necessary and will see us through to the end.

When you walk away from God and His Word, you forfeit all of the good plans He had for you.

Fear nothing and trust God for everything.

Keep a servant's heart and wait on God.

Adversity is a given but growth is optional.

God will heal every place you are hurting.

If there is no adversity there is no growth.

Aim for excellence not perfection.

You have to have a clear reception in the midst of adversity.

The enemy likes to throw static in the game.

Triumph over trauma.

It is important to heal.

Get clarity and live.

Love yourself more today than you did on yesterday.

Peace of mind is a mental state of calmness.

Cindy Isler

Spirituality reassures an order to things and generally encourages optimism and the pursuit of a joyful life.

Adversity should breed creativity.

Turn your pain into purpose.

Be obedient and birth what God has impregnated you with.

Look adversity in the face and smile.

You are a winner.

God is always rocking with you no matter what it feels like.

Be Strong

We all have had moments when we wanted to throw our hands up and walk away. Don't give up, and don't give in. God wants us to live in the now. As we endure, God changes us. We become more loving, kind and patient. We become more like Christ, which is awesome and should be encouraging to you.

The Holy Spirit shapes us through our trials. God will give you a certain richness and strength if you just stay the course. God has an amazing plan for each of us. There is work to be done!

Cindy Isler

Listening to God

God's guidance is of no value if you don't listen to Him. We all need divine guidance. God's primary way of speaking to us is through the bible. In your prayer time, how much time do you spend listening to God?

You must give God time to speak during your prayer time. He speaks through circumstances. Listening is the key! Before you start telling God about everything you are going through, try to listen to Him first. Welcome God into your situation.

Proverbs 3:5-6 *Trust in the Lord with all thine heart and lean not unto thine own understanding. In all thy ways acknowledge him, and he shall direct thy paths.* (KJV)

When God speaks it goes hand in hand with the Word of God, and He speaks quietly. It doesn't matter what anyone else thinks. It will always be clear, and He doesn't beat around the bush.

Some of the things that God says to us may clash with our flesh. Tune your heart unto God because He promised in His Word that He will guide you. God knows what it takes to get your attention. Develop a listening heart.

God will wake you up during the middle of the night. Do you ever wonder why? What do you do when He does that? Do you start watching television? Do you check your social media?

Spiritual Happiness in the Midst of Adversity

Pay attention to the times that God wakes you up during the night. He may want to talk to you or you may need to talk to Him. God speaks, but we are too busy to listen. Don't be afraid of what God will say to you? God is a God of unconditional love. He is God and He wants His one on one time with you. Be quiet before praying. Repent of your sins and turn your life over to Christ.

Jeremiah 33:3 *Call to me and I will answer you and tell you great and unsearchable things you do not know.'* (NIV)

Jeremiah 29:12 *Then you will call on me and come and pray to me, and I will listen to you.* (NIV)

Proverbs 16:20 *Whoever gives heed to instruction prospers, and blessed is the one who trusts in the Lord.* (NIV)

James 1:22 *Do not merely listen to the word, and so deceive yourselves. Do what it says.* (NIV)

Matthew 7:24 *Therefore everyone who hears these words of mine and puts them into practice is like a wise man who built his house on the rock.* (NIV)

Philippians 4:9 *Whatever you have learned or received or heard from me, or seen in me—put it into practice. And the God of peace will be with you.* (NIV)

1 John 5:15 *And if we know that he hears us— whatever we ask—we know that we have what we asked of him.* (NIV)

Romans 10:17 *Consequently, faith comes from hearing the message, and the message is heard through the word about Christ.* (NIV)

Malachi 2:2 *"If you do not listen, and if you do not resolve to honor my name," says the Lord Almighty, "I will send a curse on you, and I will curse your blessings. Yes, I have already cursed them, because you have not resolved to honor me."* (NIV)

Psalm 34:15 *The eyes of the Lord are on the righteous,*
and his ears are attentive to their cry. (NIV)

Luke 12:3 *What you have said in the dark will be heard in the daylight, and what you have whispered in the ear in the inner rooms will be proclaimed from the roofs.* (NIV)

Prayer

Thank You God, for who You are. Lord, make me a listening vessel. Please make us a listening post for people who are seeking Godly advice. Forgive me for not giving You a chance to speak during my prayer time. In Jesus name I pray. Amen.

Cindy Isler

I Will Not Quit

We all are in the process of transforming. Don't allow the habits of your past to stop you. Renew the new you and let go of the old you. Have the desire to evolve and do something different. The battle is in your mind so stop wasting your weapons on people. You will never be defeated by what people say about you. Instead, ask yourself what does God say about you?

Go after the things you want with strength. The greatness in you is overflowing. Don't allow adversity to defeat you. Be committed to what God has put inside of you. Be committed to your dreams and visions.

You will shed tears and endure struggles, but you must continue to press on. Don't give up on your dream! Even if you don't have everything you need to reach your goals at that time, don't cave in and quit. Things will turn around.

Everything in life won't always make sense, and that is ok. You go through development in the tough times. Your goal should be to come out better than before, stronger, more durable and wiser. At some point and time you will become a teacher to someone else, as there will be lessons learned as God brings you out of adversities.

Grow through everything you go through. Pain prepares you for your future. Know that your pain will pass! Let Go of the negativity, hurt and disappointment, and so on.

Spiritual Happiness in the Midst of Adversity

God redeems the time you spent in the midst of your adversity.

The enemy comes at you harder the closer you get to your dreams. Stay grounded. Plant your seeds and keep watering them. It is your time to bloom and elevate. Break free of what holds you down. Break free of that job that's holding you back. Break free of that bad relationship or addiction. Whatever it is that holds you back, break free from it.

You owe it to yourself to win so don't resist change. Everything is not going to be in order. God still works in the midst of chaos. So many things are born in the midst of a mess and out of the mess comes your message. Don't leave this life with regrets and don't let anyone tell you that you can't do what God has told you that you can.

Earlier I mentioned I love a good challenge. When someone says to me *I can't*, I laugh and tell *myself yes I can and yes I will*. When the enemy says I can't, I definitely laugh and tell him yes I can. When the enemy tells me I won't I tell him that I will. You have to be bold in your conversation with the enemy. Do not allow the enemy to punk you. Remember he has just as much power as you give him.

There have been numerous times when family and friends have tried to deter me from making my next moves, or birthing my dreams and visions. You have to get to a point in your life where you don't care what people think of you, or even what they say about you. This is between you and God, so they won't get it.

Cindy Isler

If God has put a vision, dream or idea inside of you, He will not let you let it go. It will keep you up at night and you will constantly think about it.

As I write this book adversity surrounds me constantly, but it does not stop me. It does not stop me because I refuse to give up and cave in. I refuse to let adversity win. What I will do is allow it to strengthen me as I am determined to grow through all that I am going through.

As I put my makeup on in the mornings I engage in a full blown conversation with myself, to encourage myself and empower myself. As I think about it, it is funny to me because you would think someone was literally standing right there with me. I speak life over my situations, not death. I shall live and not die to declare the works of the Lord.

Things that have laid dormant inside of you will surface because of adversities. If the adversity had not shown its face, would you have known that these things were lying there? My answer would be probably not. The bottom line is don't allow your dreams and ideas to die with you. Live your life with a sense of urgency because it is so uncertain. Don't allow your inner doubt talk you out of anything because you will be very disappointed with yourself. Trust the path that God has set before you, trust the process, but most of all, trust God.

Spiritual Happiness in the Midst of Adversity

Cindy Isler

What does the Bible say about quitting? The Bible commands us not to quit, even when we get that defeated feeling. Scripture uses the word "endure" when describing how to deal with that feeling, meaning to abide under or to stand up courageously under suffering.

And let us not grow weary of doing good, for in due season we will reap, if we do not give up" (Galatians 6:9).

Write below what you know and your experience with quitting.

Spiritual Happiness in the Midst of Adversity

Cindy Isler

Learn more from the list of Bible verses about quitting on the next few pages!

Spiritual Happiness in the Midst of Adversity

Be Strong

Psalm 31:24 *Be of good courage, and He shall strengthen your heart, all ye that hope in the LORD.* (KJV)

1 Corinthians 16:13 *Be on the alert, stand firm in the faith, act like men, be strong. (NASB)*

Philippians 4:13 *I can do all things through Christ which strengthened me. (KJV)*

2 Chronicles 15:7 *But as for you, be strong and do not give up, for your work will be rewarded.* (NIV)

Psalm 28:7 *The LORD is my strength and my shield; my heart trusted in Him, and I am helped: therefore my heart greatly rejoiceth; and with my song will I praise Him.* KJV)

Cindy Isler

Trust

Proverbs 3:5-6 *Trust in the Lord with all thine heart; and lean not unto thine own understanding. In all thy ways acknowledge Him, and He shall direct thy paths. (KJV)*

Isaiah 26:4 *Trust in the LORD forever, for the LORD, the LORD Himself, is the Rock eternal. (NIV)*

Psalm 112:6-7 *Surely the righteous will never be shaken; they will be remembered forever. They will have no fear of bad news; their hearts are steadfast, trusting in the LORD. (NIV)*

Psalm 37:5 *Commit your way to the Lord; trust in Him and He will do this. (NIV)*

There is Nothing He Can't Do Why Are You Worried?

Matthew 19:26 *But Jesus beheld them, and said unto them, "With men this is impossible; but with God all things are possible." (KJV)*

Jeremiah 32:17 *Ah, Sovereign LORD, You have made the heavens and the earth by Your great power and outstretched arm. Nothing is too hard for You. (NIV)*

Job 42:2 *I know that You can do all things; no purpose of Yours can be thwarted. (NIV)*

Cindy Isler

God Will Not Forsake You

Hebrews 13:5-6 *Keep your lives free from the love of money and be content with what you have, because God has said, "Never will I leave you; never will I forsake you." So we say with confidence, "The Lord is my helper; I will not be afraid. What can mere mortals do to me? (NIV)*

Deuteronomy 31:8 *The LORD himself goes before you and will be with you; He will never leave you nor forsake you. Do not be afraid; do not be discouraged. (NIV)*

Romans 8:32 *He that spared not his own Son, but delivered him up for us all, how shall he not with him also freely give us all things? (KJV)*

2 Corinthians 4:8-12 *We are hard pressed on every side, but not crushed; perplexed, but not in despair; persecuted, but not abandoned; struck down, but not destroyed. We always carry around in our body the death of Jesus, so that the life of Jesus may also be revealed in our body. For we who are alive are always being given over to death for Jesus' sake, so that His life may also be revealed in our mortal body. So then, death is at work in us, but life is at work in you. (NIV)*

Trials

James 1:2-4 Consider it pure joy, my brothers and sisters, whenever you face trials of many kinds, because you know that the testing of your faith produces perseverance. Let perseverance finish its work so that you may be mature and complete, not lacking anything. (NIV)

2 Corinthians 4:16-18 Therefore we do not lose heart. Though outwardly we are wasting away, yet inwardly we are being renewed day by day. For our light and momentary troubles are achieving for us an eternal glory that far outweighs them all. So we fix our eyes not on what is seen, but on what is unseen, since what is seen is temporary, but what is unseen is eternal. (NIV)

Cindy Isler

Prayer

Psalm 55:22 Cast your cares on the Lord and He will sustain you; He will never let the righteous be shaken. (NIV)

1 Thessalonians 5:16-18 Rejoice always, pray continually, give thanks in all circumstances; for this is God's will for you in Christ Jesus. (NIV)

Hebrews 11:6 And without faith it is impossible to please Him, for whoever would draw near to God must believe that He exists and that He rewards those who seek Him. (ESV)

Reminders

Romans 5:5 And hope does not put us to shame, because God's love has been poured out into our hearts through the Holy Spirit, who has been given to us. (NIV)

Romans 8:28 And we know that all things work together for good to them that love God, to them who are the called according to His purpose. (ESV)

Galatians 6:9 Let us not become weary in doing good, for at the proper time we will reap a harvest if we do not give up. (NIV)

Philippians 4:19 And my God will meet all your needs according to the riches of His glory in Christ Jesus. (NIV)

Cindy Isler

I Am Victorious

    Regardless of what you may be going through at this time in your life, cast all your cares upon the Lord. He is upholding you with His righteous right hand. Let Go of what you are refusing to lay at the foot of the cross, and once you lay it there, do not pick it up again.

    Casting your burdens upon the Lord means you have surrendered. Once you have done that you have given God full control. How much more power would you have if you turned everything over to God? It is just a question to give you something more to think about.

Prayer

Thank You God, for preserving me, and giving me endurance in the midst of adversity. I lay all my cares, burdens and fears at the foot of the cross. I would not have come out victorious if it were not for You. I thank You for working everything out for my good. In Jesus name, I pray! Amen and Amen.

Cindy Isler

Straight From My Heart

I have cried. I have prayed. I have been misunderstood. I have waited on God. I have followed the Holy Spirit's promptings. I have gone left when God said go right. I have laid on my face in my prayer closet. I have sat in silence waiting to hear from the God. He has called my name with His still small voice during the midnight hour. He has tapped me on my side to wake me up. God has placed people in my life to pour into me.

God has sent me what I needed in order for me to get to my next levels in life so that He can get all of the glory. I have been lied on, relationships have been dissolved and new ones have been created.

I wanted to share these things with you because I too have been through a lot of adversity and pain. BUT GOD and only God has sustained me and brought me through the fire unburned. It is important that you know that everything you go through is for a reason. God will never ever abandon you no matter what chapter of your life you are in. Keep God's promises in your heart and in your mouth.

Spiritual Happiness in the Midst of Adversity

On this page, take the time to be honest and share straight from your heart. What are some things that helped you get through adversity, difficulties and pain? What could you have done differently?

Cindy Isler

Spiritual Happiness in the Midst of Adversity

Prayer

    Heavenly Father, I just want to thank You for being You, because if it weren't for You, there would be no me. I thank You for trusting me enough to write this book and share wisdom with Your children. I ask that You cover everyone that reads this book and that it will be a blessing to them in some way.

    I pray that Your children learn from the lessons during these situations. I pray that they grow and mature in Your word. I pray that they don't feel like You have abandoned them or that they are being punished. I pray that the stories in this book will encourage and empower them.

    I want to thank You for the adversities that I have gone through. I want to thank You for healing me mentally, physically and spiritually. God, You have kept me covered in every situation that I had to endure. Every adversity is continuing to help me become the woman of God I am and disciple that You are calling me to be.

    I know that I am rendered less than perfect, and I am thankful for that. If I were perfect, I would not need You as much, so I welcome my flaws and imperfections. The best part of it all is that I am still wonderfully made, and that I am Your masterpiece.

    Thank You, for being the potter knowing that I am the clay. Thank You for keeping Your hands on me to shape and mold me. I know that You are not finished with me yet and that this is part of the process.

I welcome all the bountiful blessings that You have for me. I thank You that I am a blessing to countless people. I thank You for the capacity to do what You are calling me to do. I choose triumph over adversity, I choose clarity over chaos, I choose purpose over pain.

I know nothing overrides Your promises, God, and that there is a word from You to help us get through everything we go through. So Heavenly Father, thank You, thank You, thank You for just loving me and wrapping Your loving arms around me. In Jesus' name I pray. From my mouth to Your ears. Amen and Amen

www.ingramcontent.com/pod-product-compliance
Lightning Source LLC
Chambersburg PA
CBHW070313100426
42743CB00011B/2445